American Battlefields

LEXINGTON AND CONCORD

APRIL 19, 1775

Dale Anderson

ENCHANTED LION BOOKS
New York

© 2004 White-Thomson Publishing Limited
and Enchanted Lion Books LLC

Published in the United States of America in 2004 by
Enchanted Lion Books, 115 West 18 St., 6 fl, New York, NY 10011

Library of Congress Cataloging-in-Publication Data

Anderson, Dale, 1953-

Lexington and Concord, April 19, 1775 / Dale Anderson.

p. cm.— (American battlefields)

Includes bibliographical references and index.

ISBN 1-59270-027-6

1. Lexington, Battle of, Lexington, Mass., 1775—Juvenile literature.
2. Concord, Battle of, Concord, Mass., 1775—Juvenile literature. [1.
Lexington, Battle of, Lexington, Mass., 1775. 2. Concord, Battle of,
Concord, Mass., 1775. 3. United States—History—Revolution,
1775-1783—Campaigns.] I. Title. II. Series.

E241.L6A53 2004

973.3'311—dc22   2003071037

Created for Enchanted Lion Books by

White-Thomson Publishing Limited

Bridgewater Business Centre

210 High Sreet

Lewes BN7 2UH

Titles in the series American Battlefields:

The Alamo

Gettysburg

Lexington and Concord

Little Bighorn

Editorial Credits

Editor: Peg Goldstein

Design: Malcolm Walker, based on a series design by Jamie Asher

Consultant: Steve Mills, Ph.D., Keele University

Proofreader: Alison Cooper

Picture Research: John Klein

Artwork: Peter Bull Studio

Enchanted Lion Books

Editor: Claudia Zoe Bedrick

Production: Millicent Fairhurst

Printed in China by South China Printing Company

Picture Credits:

Concord Museum, Concord, MA, www.concordmuseum.org 13(b), 22;
Corbis 13, 15, 16; I. N. Phelps Stokes Collection, Miriam and Ira D.
Wallace Division of Art, Prints, and Photographs, New York Public
Library, Lennox and Tilden Foundations 12; Lexington Historical
Society 14, 24; Library of Congress 6, 25; National Guard Bureau
(painting © Don Troiani) cover, 19(t); Peabody Essex Museum 19(b);
Peter Newark title page, imprint page, 5, 7(t), 7(b), 8, 9(t), 9(b), 10,
11(t), 11(b), 18, 20, 21, 23, 24(b), 26, 27, 28(t), 28(b), 30–31.

Cover art: A painting of the Battle of Lexington © Don Troiani. Courtesy
of National Guard Bureau.

Title page art: Battle of Lexington 19 April, 1775, engraved by
eyewitness Amos Dolittle. Peter Newark's American Pictures.

CONTENTS

SEEDS OF A REVOLUTION

O N APRIL 19, 1775, colonists fought British soldiers at Lexington and then Concord, Massachusetts. These two battles, little more than skirmishes, were small, involving only a few hundred soldiers on both sides. But they were important. They launched the American Revolution— the fight for American independence.

When the two battles were over, America was still a series of colonies, or settlements, controlled by Great Britain. Most colonists were happy with this arrangement. Only a small number wanted independence. But the two battles—and the new attitudes they fostered—helped persuade many Americans that they should break with Great Britain. The battles of Lexington and Concord helped start the Revolution. But the seeds of that revolution had been planted many years before.

In the early 1600s, Great Britain and France began establishing colonies in North America. Britain's colonies hugged the Atlantic coast. France controlled present-day eastern Canada, the Great Lakes, and the Mississippi River valley. Britain and France fought several wars trying to gain the other's colonies. Britain won the last of these wars in 1763 and took over France's North American colonies east of the Mississippi.

But this victory gave the British government a problem. It had borrowed large sums of money to pay for the war. It also needed to place more troops in North America because now it had more land to defend. These soldiers not only had to protect the western outpost of the British Empire but also had to protect colonists from Native Americans, whose ancestors had lived in the Americas for thousands of years.

The original thirteen colonies ran along the eastern coast of North America. Native American lands lay to the west.

This painting shows French general Montcalm victorious at Ticonderoga in 1758, during the costly French and Indian War (1754–1763).

Native Americans sometimes attacked the colonists, who were pushing out from the coast and taking over more and more or their land.

The British government felt that the colonists should pay some of these expenses. After all, the colonists benefited from the end of French rule and from protection against Native American attacks. Starting in 1764, the British Parliament, or legislature, passed several laws raising taxes in the colonies.

THIRTEEN COLONIES

The first permanent British colony in the Americas was Jamestown, Virginia, established in 1607. In the 1620s and 1630s, colonists settled farther north, primarily in New England. Over the years, the British created thirteen colonies, stretching from New Hampshire down to Georgia.

Most colonists came from England, with only some from Scotland, Ireland, and numerous other European nations. Some came to take advantage of the large amount of cheap land in North America. Others came for religious freedom—they wanted to worship as they chose—a freedom they didn't have in Europe.

By the 1770s, the British colonies in North America had about 2.5 million inhabitants. About 400,000 of those people were of African descent, most of them slaves. They had been brought from Africa against their will to work on American farms. Most slaves lived in the southern colonies.

NO TAXATION WITHOUT REPRESENTATION

Many colonists met the new taxes with angry protests. They saw the taxes as a dramatic change in British rule. For many years, the British had mostly let the colonies govern and tax themselves. The colonies had prospered and enjoyed peace. Now, the colonists believed, Parliament was passing laws that interfered with their lives. They also thought these laws ignored their rights as British subjects. Colonists pointed out that none of them were members of Parliament. Therefore, they said, the laws had been made without their consent. Leaders such as Samuel Adams spurred these protests. He organized a group called the Sons of Liberty.

The Sons of Liberty started in Boston, Massachusetts, but it eventually spread to other colonies. Its members campaigned against the new British tax laws, protesting in many different ways. Some members wrote newspaper articles and books criticizing the laws. Others promised not to buy any of the goods being taxed. That way, the British government could not collect as much tax money. Some Sons of Liberty attacked tax collectors, shouting angry words at them, at times covering them with sticky tar and feathers. Sometimes they rioted. To "Loyalists," colonists still loyal to Great Britain, such actions seemed worse than the problems about which the Sons of Liberty were protesting.

The protests made British leaders more and more angry. The government insisted that Parliament had every right to tax the colonies. Because the colonists were British subjects, British leaders said, they had to obey laws passed by Parliament. Parliament passed new laws that further restricted business and local government in the colonies. These new laws caused new protests.

In 1770 the anger erupted into violence. On March 5, an unruly mob harassed some British soldiers on a street in Boston.

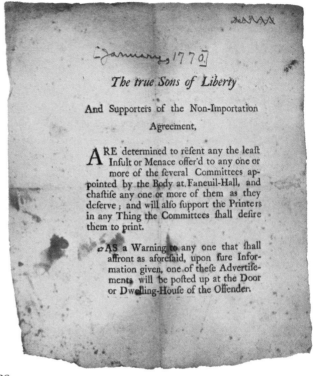

Using articles, letters, and decrees, the Sons of Liberty spread their ideas throughout the thirteen colonies.

> *"Every act of oppression will sour [the colonists'] tempers, lessen greatly if not annihilate the profits of your commerce with them, and hasten their final revolt: for the seeds of liberty are universally sown there."[1]*
> —American statesman Benjamin Franklin, warning the British about the tax laws

Patriot Paul Revere made this engraving of the Boston Massacre. Although the engraving was inaccurate, it helped persuade many colonists to oppose British rule.

The soldiers, fearing for their safety, fired into the crowd. Five colonists were killed. Enraged colonists called the event the Boston Massacre. Samuel Adams and his supporters published articles and pictures that portrayed the British soldiers as bloodthirsty tyrants. Ironically, the same day as the massacre, Parliament was moving to calm the colonies down. It repealed all the taxes enacted in 1767, except the one on tea.

THE FATHER OF THE SONS OF LIBERTY

Boston's Samuel Adams was not a good businessman. He inherited a brewery, but his bad business sense left him in debt and poor. What he cared about was politics. He held various offices in the governments of Massachusetts and Boston. More important, he worked behind the scenes to organize protests against the British. Adams was one of the first colonists to believe that the Americans should try to win independence from Great Britain.

A TEA PARTY

TEA, ONE ITEM the British taxed, was a popular drink in the American colonies. To protest the tax, many colonists stopped buying British tea. Some colonists bought tea from other countries illegally. Meanwhile, a large British company that controlled the tea trade was close to going out of business. To save this important company, Parliament passed a new law allowing only British merchants, not those of the colonies, to distribute tea in the colonies. Samuel Adams and his Sons of Liberty struck back. On December 16, 1773, a mob of colonists marched onto a British ship docked at Boston. They dumped its crates of tea into the harbor, an event called the Boston Tea Party.

This act outraged many people in Britain, even more than earlier protests had. After all, the colonists had willfully destroyed property to defy the law. British leaders decided to punish the colonists, especially those in Boston and Massachusetts. They pushed four tough laws through Parliament. The laws were called the Coercive Acts because they were meant to coerce, or force, the colonists to obey British authority.

Wearing Native American headdresses, colonists snuck onto a British ship and dumped 342 crates of tea into the harbor.

"The colonies must either submit or triumph. I do not wish to come to severe measures, but we must not retreat. By coolness and [firm] pursuit of the [laws] that have been adopted I trust that they will come to submit."[2]
—King George III of Britain, remarking on the Coercive Acts

The first law closed the port of Boston. The second law put the British in greater control of local government in Massachusetts. The third said that colonists charged with certain crimes would be tried in Britain, not in the colonies. The fourth said that people in Boston had to allow British soldiers to live in their homes and inns.

It was the colonists' turn to be outraged. Closing the port threw many people out of work. Losing control of local government took away their basic rights as free people. Many Americans blasted the laws, calling them Intolerable Acts. Anger spread throughout the colonies. People outside Massachusetts feared that the harsh actions against Boston could be taken against them, too.

Meanwhile, the British government named a new governor for the colony of Massachusetts. He was Thomas Gage, a British general. He arrived in Boston in May 1774 to take charge. He was determined to be tough with the rebellious colonists.

In Britain, King George III was determined to crush American resistance.

THE HEAD OF THE BRITISH FORCES

Thomas Gage was the younger son of a British nobleman who had little money. Forced to make his own way in the world, Gage entered the army. By the 1750s he had risen to the rank of colonel. He took part in the French and Indian War, the fight in which Britain won France's colonies. As a reward for his service, Gage was made a general and put in command of all British forces in North America.

ORGANIZED RESISTANCE

The colonists weren't all in agreement about their relationship to Great Britain. The Loyalists supported the British, come what may. They were upset by the protests, riots, and unrest. Those who opposed the British came to be called Patriots. At first they were the smallest group.

A third group was still loyal to Britain but was growing increasingly angry over the British government's actions. Some in this group thought they could appeal to the British king, George III, to stop the unpopular laws passed by Parliament. But as Britain took harsher and harsher measures against the colonists, many in this group eventually joined the Patriot cause.

Very few colonists believed the American colonies should go so far as seeking independence from Britain. One who did was Samuel Adams, and he worked to gain more support for the idea. He got groups of Patriots in different places talking—and working—together. He persuaded the Boston city government to put several Patriots on a Committee of Correspondence. Its task was to publish articles protesting British actions. Committee members also sent letters to Patriots in other towns and colonies. Patriot Paul Revere worked closely with Adams and other Patriot leaders, including a man named John Hancock, and carried many of their letters.

"[The Coercive Acts are] glaring evidence of a fixed plan of the British administration to bring the whole continent into the most humiliating bondage."[3]
—Boston Committee of Correspondence

Silversmith Paul Revere became a Patriot hero.

★ SILVERSMITH TURNED PATRIOT

Paul Revere, following his father, became a silversmith, a person who makes silver objects such as bowls and utensils. He also got involved in politics. He was an important figure in the Patriot cause because he linked two groups. He worked closely with leaders such as Samuel Adams and John Hancock, but he also worked with common people such as laborers and shop owners. Revere was the chief messenger for the Patriots. He regularly carried messages from Adams and Hancock to leaders in other towns and colonies, going as far as Pennsylvania and New Hampshire on horseback.

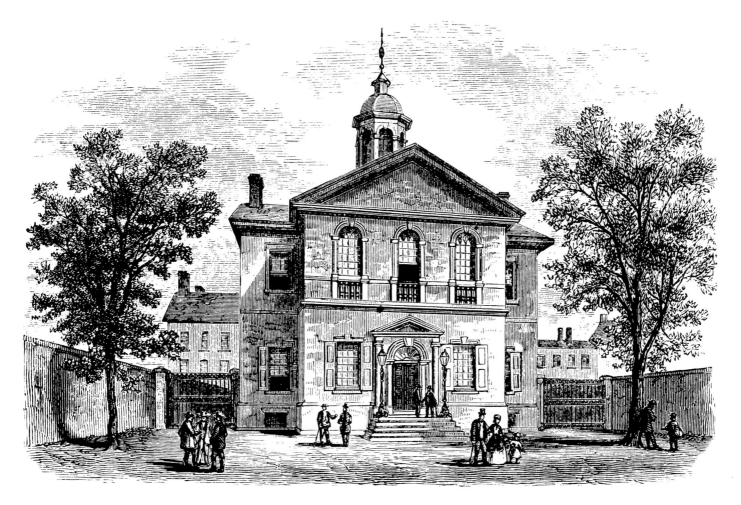

Carpenters' Hall in Philadelphia, site of the First Continental Congress.

In September 1774, Patriot leaders met in Philadelphia, Pennsylvania, to discuss their plans. Every colony but Georgia sent representatives to the meeting. Called the First Continental Congress, the meeting lasted about six weeks. The Congress called on each colony to form militias, or armies of citizen soldiers. It urged people to refuse to buy British goods, hoping to hurt Britain's economy. Finally, it decided to meet again the following spring to consider further actions if the British government did not change its policies.

Towns across the colonies formed militia companies. They began gathering guns, gunpowder, and bullets. Some of these supplies were stolen from British forts.

Patriot John Hancock would become famous as the first person to sign the Declaration of Independence.

11

TALK BECOMES ACTION

Militia companies around Boston began training in earnest. General Gage worried about these forces. He sent troops to towns near Boston to seize the colonists' supplies. After one such raid, 4,000 militiamen gathered in nearby Cambridge in a show of force. Gage grew more alarmed.

While townspeople look on, British troops drill and march on Boston Common.

WHO WAS THE SPY?

Both Gage and the Patriots worked hard to keep their plans secret, but each had a good idea of what the other side was doing. Gage received reports from Loyalists. Meanwhile, Revere's network of ordinary workers reported on the movements of Gage's soldiers. The Patriots also had a spy planted very close to Gage.
On April 18 that spy confirmed that British troops were going to Concord. No one knows the identity of the spy, but some evidence suggests it was Gage's wife.

Another British raid was less successful—but more alarming. When British soldiers arrived in Salem, Massachusetts, to seize military supplies there, hundreds of colonists swarmed into the streets to stop them. In a tense meeting that might have resulted in bloodshed, the British backed down. They returned to Boston without taking anything. The incident showed that the colonists had little respect for the British soldiers—and no fear of them.

Thinking that the situation was growing worse, Gage asked for, and received, more troops. By April 1775 he had 4,000 soldiers in Boston. He also had new orders from the British government to move against the Patriots. His commanders told him, "The King's dignity and the honor and safety of the Empire require that . . . force should be repelled with force."[4]

On April 18, Gage developed his plans. He wanted a large body of troops to seize Patriot guns and ammunition in Concord, about twenty miles from Boston. The soldiers were also to capture Sam Adams and John Hancock in nearby Lexington.

William Dawes took the southern route to Concord.

> "I agreed with a Colonel Conant . . . that if the British went out by water, we would show two [lanterns] in the North Church steeple, and if by land, one."[5]
> —Paul Revere

Dr. Joseph Warren, another Patriot leader, learned of Gage's plans. He told Paul Revere to warn Adams and Hancock. In case British troops stopped Revere, he told another rider, William Dawes, to carry the warning by a different route.

The Patriots weren't sure how the British would get to Concord. Would they march from Boston to Concord from the south, by land? Or would they take a northerly route, first crossing the Charles River? The route they took would affect how much time the Patriots had to respond. Revere arranged for another Patriot to put lanterns in the steeple of a Boston church. The lanterns would serve as a signal to tell colleagues across the river in Charlestown which route the British were taking. These Patriots had instructions to send a third messenger in case the British stopped both Revere and Dawes.

One of the two lanterns lit in the steeple of the Old North Church, signaling that the British were on the northern route.

BRITISH PLANS

GAGE PUT TOGETHER a force of about 800 soldiers. In command was Lieutenant Colonel Francis Smith. Major John Pitcairn, a tough soldier, was put in charge of the advance guard, which marched in front of the main body of soldiers. But Smith and Pitcairn were not used to working with the soldiers they commanded on this expedition. This unfamiliarity would hurt the British.

Gage's scouts had told him that the southern route, the main road from Boston to Concord, was not safe. The road was long, and it was dangerous because hills stood on either side of it. Patriot militiamen could easily attack the British from those hills. The scouts recommended crossing the Charles River into Cambridge and then taking a northern route. Gage told Smith and Pitcairn to follow this advice.

At about 10:00 p.m. on April 18, the British troops began to move. Soon after, William Dawes started his ride. He took the main road, the southern route to Concord. He had a slow horse and had to avoid British patrols. It took him about three hours to reach Lexington.

Major John Pitcairn was an experienced British officer.

As the British set out for Lexington, Revere and Dawes, trying to evade enemy patrols, set out as well.

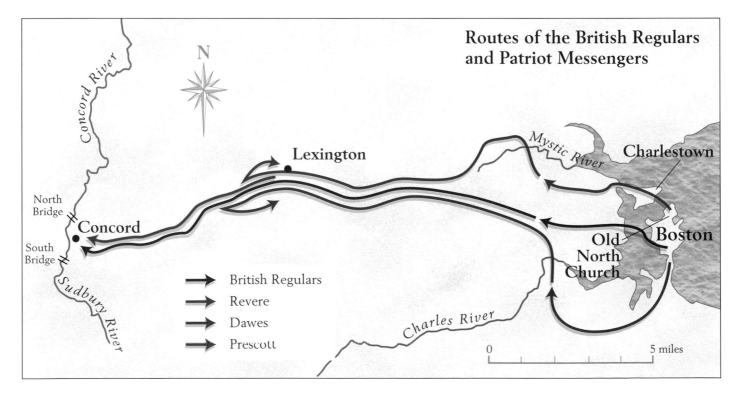

Routes of the British Regulars and Patriot Messengers

N

Concord River

Lexington

Mystic River

Charlestown

North Bridge

Concord

South Bridge

Old North Church

Boston

Sudbury River

Charles River

→ British Regulars
→ Revere
→ Dawes
→ Prescott

0   5 miles

At the same time, Revere had his friends light two lanterns in the steeple of the Old North Church, signaling that the British were taking the river route. The Patriots in Charlestown sent out another rider, as they had agreed to do.

Meanwhile, Revere prepared for his own trip to Concord. Friends rowed him across the Charles River. In Charlestown he picked up a fast horse named Brown Beauty and began his ride. On his way to Lexington, he had to avoid British patrols, outracing one group to escape capture. He stopped at many towns, telling Patriot leaders that the British were on the march. Those leaders sent out other riders to spread the alarm.

At about midnight, Revere reached the Lexington house where Adams and Hancock were staying. They, and the family hosting them, were all asleep. A militia sergeant standing guard outside the house told Revere to keep down the noise so that he would not disturb the family. "Noise!" Revere answered, "You'll have noise enough before long! The Regulars [British soldiers] are coming out!"[6]

About half an hour later, Dawes also reached Lexington. The rider from Charlestown never made it. He was probably captured by British patrols.

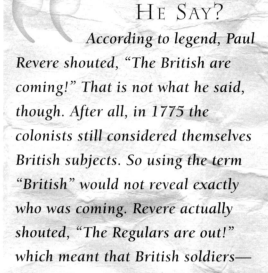

WHAT DID HE SAY?

According to legend, Paul Revere shouted, "The British are coming!" That is not what he said, though. After all, in 1775 the colonists still considered themselves British subjects. So using the term "British" would not reveal exactly who was coming. Revere actually shouted, "The Regulars are out!" which meant that British soldiers— men of the regular army—were on the march.

Revere and Brown Beauty ride for Lexington.

THE ROAD TO LEXINGTON

While Dawes and Revere rode to Lexington, the British regulars were moving. Their march began badly. The boats carrying them across the river ran aground, and the soldiers had to slog through mud to the shore. Moreover, there weren't enough boats to carry them all at once. The first soldiers across had to stand, wet and cold in the chilly night, waiting for the boats to bring the rest of the force. Finally, at about 2:00 in the morning, they set out for Lexington. The march took a few hours.

Meanwhile, warned by Revere, the Lexington militiamen had gathered on the town green, an open space located in the center of most New England towns. There were fewer than eighty of them, ranging in age from sixteen to sixty-six. Their commander was Captain John Parker, a farmer. While the men waited, he sent out scouts to look for the British. One returned, having seen no sign of soldiers. Parker dismissed the men but told them to stay nearby.

Revere and Dawes had left for Concord to warn the militia there. On the way, they met Dr. Samuel Prescott, another Patriot. He joined them, but the three riders ran into a British patrol. Prescott got away and was the only one to actually reach Concord. Dawes lost his horse but hid in the bushes. Revere was caught and questioned. The British took his horse but released him. Revere walked back to Lexington. Upon arriving, he was surprised to see Adams and Hancock still in town. He convinced them they had to go. Just before dawn, they finally left.

> *"What we meant in going for those Redcoats was this: we always had governed ourselves and we always meant to. They didn't mean we should."*[7]
> —Levi Preston, colonial militiaman

Bedford, located between Lexington and Concord to the north, had a minuteman division. This was its flag.

THE MINUTEMEN

In 1774, as tension between colonists and the British increased, one county in Massachusetts organized a special militia called minutemen. These men promised to be ready to fight on a minute's notice. Other counties took up the idea. Lexington did not have minutemen, only ordinary militiamen. Some of Concord's militiamen were minutemen, however.

While all this was taking place, the British troops neared Lexington. Though the officers knew what was happening, the British soldiers had no idea what their mission was. Near Lexington, part of the force met the patrol that had caught Revere. Members of the patrol explained that Revere had been raising the alarm and that militiamen were gathering. Word quickly spread through the British force: they were on a raiding expedition, and the colonists knew they were coming.

REDCOATS AND NO COATS

British soldiers wore bright red coats, which gave them their nickname, Redcoats. The coats were made of heavy wool and had long tails stretching to the knee. Some units wore shorter red jackets. Underneath, the men wore knee-length pants and vests. Most carried a heavy musket called a Brown Bess. These guns fired lead balls that had to be loaded from the muzzle, or barrel. British soldiers were also equipped with short swords and bayonets. They carried a day's worth of food in small shoulder bags. Unlike the British, the colonial militiamen had no standard uniform. In fact, most men fought in their everyday clothes. They carried their own guns, which were muzzle-loading muskets similar to the British guns. Some carried swords. To regular troops, such ill-equipped men must have seemed little better than armed rioters, certainly not people to be taken seriously in battle. But the militiamen had the advantage of fighting in places many of them had known all their lives, not thousands of miles from home.

BATTLE!

Back in Lexington, a second militia scout returned. He confirmed that the British regulars were on the march—and said they were only half an hour away. Parker sounded the alarm, and his men gathered once again on the green. He formed them into two lines, facing east, toward the advancing British force. Several townspeople stood nearby, watching. Paul Revere was also near the green. He had returned to Lexington to get a trunk filled with important papers that Adams and Hancock had forgotten when they left.

> "[The British troops] made a short halt when I saw, and heard, a gun fired, which appeared to be a pistol. Then I could distinguish two guns, and then a continual roar of musketry."[9]
> —Paul Revere

Shortly after dawn, Major Pitcairn and his advance guard arrived. He drew his men, about 240 soldiers, into a line facing the militia and came forward on his horse. "Throw down your arms, you villains, you rebels!"[8] he ordered.

Only about 200 feet separated the two forces. There was tension in the air.

Facing a volley from John Pitcairn's advance guard, Lexington militiamen scatter.

A painting of the Battle of Lexington. Each side blamed the other for firing the first shot.

WHICH SIDE FIRED THE FIRST SHOT?

No one knows which side fired the first shot at Lexington. After the battle, both colonists and British soldiers claimed that their side did not shoot first. Many witnesses said the first shot came from behind a fence or a building. Some historians think a civilian fired this shot, perhaps on orders from Samuel Adams. They say that Adams knew the shot would provoke the British to shoot back. He could then point to the British shooting as an outrageous attack on the colonists. That would help him in his goal of pushing the colonies toward independence. Another possibility is that someone's gun went off accidentally.

Parker did not think his seventy-seven men could oppose so many troops. He told his men to let the British pass. Then, from somewhere, a shot rang out. The British suspected militiamen were firing at them and opened fire, though they had no orders to do so. Two militiamen were hit, and the rest scattered. The British lost all discipline and would not listen to the officers' orders to stop. Some ran at the colonists with bayonets flashing, wounding several of them. Some began entering nearby buildings. Then Colonel Smith arrived and managed to restore order.

The battle of Lexington was over. Seven men of Lexington were dead, and ten more were wounded. Jonathan Harrington died at the doorstep of his house, as his wife and son watched in horror. Another of the dead was Jonas Parker, a relative of the captain. Only one British soldier was wounded.

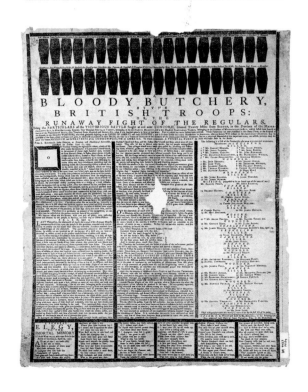

A Salem Gazette *article recounts the clash at Lexington.*

THE MARCH TO CONCORD

A FTER COLONEL SMITH restored order, he told his officers to assemble the men and begin the march to Concord. Some officers protested the order. They worried that they would face even more armed colonists at Concord. They were also upset that their own men had attacked the colonists without orders to do so. They feared the situation was getting out of hand.

Smith dismissed their fears and ordered them to march. Major Pitcairn agreed with him. The British troops emptied their weapons by firing a victory salute into the air, let out three cheers, and marched on.

Two hours later, they reached Concord. The militias from Concord and nearby Lincoln were assembled on the Concord green, but they were outnumbered by the British force. The colonists debated what to do. Some wanted to fight, but others felt the odds were against them. Also, they did not want to be the ones to start the fight. They wanted that responsibility to fall on British soldiers. The militiamen decided to pull back out of town.

With British troops massed near the town center, Pitcairn and Smith await the approaching militiamen.

Smith quickly sent troops to search homes for military supplies. The search proved largely unsuccessful. The colonists, warned of the approaching troops, had hidden most of their supplies. One farmer's sons plowed their fields, placed guns in the long rows in the ground, and then covered them over with dirt.

The British soldiers did find some musket balls, which they dumped into a pond. They also found three cannons. They burned the wooden carriages that held the cannons' barrels. This fire spread to the nearby courthouse. British soldiers joined with townspeople to put out the fire.

Smith had placed guards at two bridges leading into town. Three companies—about 115 men—stood by the North Bridge, about 800 yards from the town center. Another force was sent to defend the South Bridge.

Meanwhile, hundreds of militiamen from many towns in Massachusetts were streaming toward Concord. Some of them already knew about the fight in Lexington. More were on their way.

ORDINARY PEOPLE

The men of the Massachusetts militia were ordinary people. Most were farmers. Many were veterans of the recent war against France. The militiamen also included teenage boys who had never seen battle before. Some, like James Nichols, had recently come to America from Britain. Without the regulars' red uniforms, it would have been difficult in the heat of battle to tell friend from foe.

Some of the militiamen were of African descent. Prince Estabrook, who had been a slave, won his freedom by fighting at Lexington, where he was wounded. Peter Salem was a free black who fought at Concord. Two months later, he served at the Battle of Bunker Hill. Some accounts give him credit for killing Major John Pitcairn in that battle.

Militiamen arm themselves and leave their families to join the fight against the British.

"**The sun was rising and shined on their arms, and [the British] made a noble appearance in their red coats and glistening arms.**"[10]
—Thaddeus Blood, Concord militiaman

FIGHT AND FLIGHT

About 500 militiamen had gathered north of the North Bridge. When they saw smoke rising from the burning courthouse in Concord, they thought the British were setting fire to homes. They grew angry. Colonel James Barrett, the commander, ordered his men to load their weapons but hold their fire. Then he told the militia to advance toward the bridge.

The British troops guarding the bridge were badly outnumbered by the oncoming militia force. The officer in charge ordered his men to fall back across the bridge, on the town side of the Concord River. Suddenly—and without receiving orders to do so—a British soldier fired, and the others followed. Two militiamen were killed. Others were wounded. Most of the shots flew above the heads of the advancing force, however. The British were firing too high—a sign of their inexperience and nerves.

The militiamen kept coming, though more were killed or wounded as British fire continued. When they got within fifty yards of the British, they finally opened fire. A Concord militia officer shouted, "Fire, fellow soldiers, for God's sake fire!"[11] Shots quickly poured out of the colonists' lines. Three British privates fell dead; four officers and five soldiers were wounded. The rest of the British troops ran south to Concord.

The militia crossed the bridge. They formed a line behind a stone wall and waited.

Smith came up from town with more of his troops. Seeing the enemy protected behind the stone wall, he led his soldiers back to the Concord green. He was frustrated by the failure to find many weapons or powder. He was also worried about the gathering militiamen. At about midday, he ordered his force to return to Boston.

The British began the long march east. They covered the first mile without any difficulties. At a spot called Merriam's Corner, though, hidden militia units opened fire on them. Two British

Approaching from the hills, colonial militiamen force the British back across the North Bridge.

Right: *Militiamen fire on the retreating British column at Bloody Angle.*

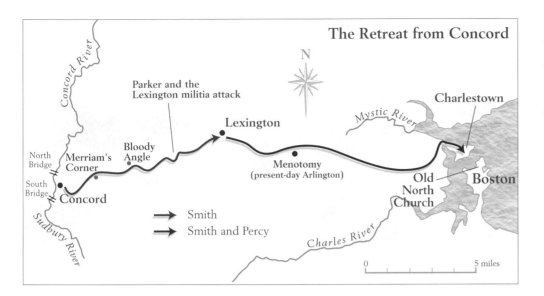

The Retreat from Concord

Concord River

N

Parker and the
Lexington militia attack

Charlestown

Mystic River

Lexington

North
Bridge

Merriam's
Corner

Bloody
Angle

Menotomy
(present-day Arlington)

South
Bridge

Concord

Smith

Smith and Percy

Sudbury River

Charles River

Old
North
Church

Boston

0   5 miles

As the British retraced their steps back to Charlestown, the militiamen went on the attack.

soldiers fell dead, and several more were wounded. When the colonists withdrew, the British marched on.

About a mile farther on, at Brooks Hill, the militia attacked once again. Here, too, British soldiers were killed and wounded before the militiamen were driven off.

Shortly after, the road turned sharply to the north. The militia ambushed the retreating army. Thirty British soldiers were killed or wounded at this spot, now called the Bloody Angle.

Farther east, the British ran into the Lexington militia. Seeking revenge, Captain Parker's men fired away, killing and wounding more regulars. Among the wounded was Colonel Smith.

"Our men had very few opportunities of getting good shots at the Rebels, as they hardly ever fired but under cover of a stone wall, from behind a tree, or out of a house; and the moment they had fired they lay down out of sight until they had loaded again."[12]
—British lieutenant Frederick MacKenzie, describing the march back to Boston

THE LONG ROAD HOME

The British soldiers were tired, hungry, and thirsty. It was afternoon, and they had been on the move since the night before. Worse, they faced new fire every few hundred yards. Some had run out of powder and musket balls. The soldiers began losing discipline. Some surrendered. Others began to run. The march was becoming a rout.

Smith's force might have completely fallen apart, but in Lexington they found relief. When Smith had learned that the militia was gathering against him, he had sent a rider galloping back to Boston, asking for reinforcements. Gage had assembled a new force of more than a thousand troops and two cannons, under the command of Lord Hugh Percy.

Percy's force set out early in the morning, around the time Smith's troops reached Concord. Some armed Loyalists marched with Percy's men. By about two in the afternoon, Percy's force reached Lexington. Hearing gunfire to the west, Percy positioned his troops and cannons on the Lexington green. Soon after, Smith's troops arrived from the west. The panicked soldiers were overjoyed to see the reinforcements.

Around mid-afternoon, the combined British force resumed the eastward march. But the militia did not let them return to Boston easily. Joseph Warren and another Patriot named William Heath had arrived on the scene and taken charge. Heath developed a plan to keep up the attacks, bringing in fresh troops

Lord Hugh Percy arrived to assist Smith's retreating troops.

EARL PERCY,   A.D.1775

❝ *"Nor will the insurrection here turn out so [minor] as it is perhaps imagined at home. For my part, I never believed, I confess, that they [would] have attacked the king's troops, or have had the perseverance I found in them yesterday."*[13]
—Lord Hugh Percy

JOIN, or DIE.

Benjamin Franklin created this rattlesnake cartoon to urge the colonies to unite to fight the French and Indian War. The Americans revived the cartoon when the Revolution began.

to hit the British from both sides and the rear. Percy said the militia "followed us wherever we went"[14] all the way back to Boston.

At the town of Menotomy, the British struck back. They entered some homes, looking for enemies in hiding. Along with killing militiamen, they killed civilians and burned houses. As rebel leaders such as Sam Adams had been saying to their Patriot supporters, the British troops were increasingly acting like an army of occupation, rather than defenders of the community.

By early evening, the British had finally reached safety in Charlestown. The men dropped to the ground, exhausted. The battles of Lexington and Concord were over.

British losses had been heavy—65 killed, 180 wounded, and nearly 30 missing. Many of the wounded were officers. The militia had made sure to target them. The militia had suffered far less, with 50 dead and 39 wounded. Most importantly, British regular soldiers had been shown to be extremely vulnerable to guerrilla warfare in increasingly hostile territory.

★ JOSEPH WARREN

Handsome, educated, and a skilled doctor, Joseph Warren was a leading figure in Boston. He was also a very active Patriot. After Lexington and Concord, Warren was made a militia general. He helped command forces that fought the British at the Battle of Bunker Hill in June 1775. He was killed in that battle.

THE AMERICAN REVOLUTION

PATRIOT LEADERS QUICKLY spread the news of the battles to other towns in Massachusetts and to other colonies. By May 9 word had reached as far as South Carolina. Patriot leaders did not tell the whole story, however—and they stretched the truth. They wanted the battles to look like a case of heroic civilians fighting against cruel invaders. They did not mention the warning riders. They blamed the British for shooting first in Lexington, even though the truth about that situation was unclear. They emphasized stories of British soldiers hurting civilians and burning homes. These accounts fanned anger against the British government and convinced more people to join the Patriot cause.

In May 1775, colonial leaders again gathered in Philadelphia, holding the Second Continental Congress. The representatives at the meeting heard the grim news about Lexington and Concord. They called on the colonists to form a new army. Soon after, the Congress assigned George Washington to command the military forces. He quickly went to Massachusetts to take charge. The conflict had turned into a full-scale war. The first major fight between the British and colonists took place in June at the Battle of Bunker Hill.

But many colonists were still unwilling to break with Britain. The Continental Congress sent a message to King George, asking him to grant the rights the colonists wanted and to stop the fighting. An angry King George refused to listen. Instead, he declared that the colonies were in rebellion and sent more troops.

This action and further warfare helped convince more colonists that the colonies should become independent. In July 1776, the Continental Congress officially declared that the colonists were forming a new country, the United States of America.

With the war for independence fully underway, George Washington took command of the colonial militias.

This famous painting by John Trumbull shows Thomas Jefferson (later president of the United States) presenting the Declaration of Independence to the Continental Congress.

As the long, bitter war continued, many Loyalists moved north to Canada or south to Jamaica, both of which remained British colonies. Some even went back to Britain. But many Loyalists stayed and made the best of it, along with the great majority of Americans.

Lexington and Concord were the first battles in a long, difficult war. The American Revolution dragged on into the 1780s. Eventually, many people in Britain grew weary of the war and its expense. The French joined in to help the Americans, eager for revenge for their earlier defeat.

Finally, a large British army surrendered to the Americans and their French allies at Yorktown, Virginia, in 1781. Yorktown was the last major battle of the war. Two years later, Britain acknowledged the United States as an independent nation.

THE DECLARATION OF INDEPENDENCE

"We . . . representatives of the United States of America . . . do . . . solemnly publish and declare, that these united colonies are, and of right ought to be free and independent states . . . and that all political connection between them and the state of Great Britain, is and ought to be totally dissolved."
—Portion of the Declaration of Independence, July 4, 1776

AFTER THE BATTLES

Over time, Americans came to see the battles of Lexington and Concord as the first steps toward American independence. In the 1830s, more than fifty years after the Revolution, people around Concord raised money to build a battle monument. In 1874 Concord dedicated a statue to the militiamen. In 1900, Lexington dedicated its own statue. Both still stand. In the late 1800s, Massachusetts made April 19 a state holiday called Patriot's Day.

In the late 1950s, the National Park Service created Minute Man National Park, which includes about 970 acres of land around Lexington and Concord. One part of the park includes the North Bridge, where the fight at Concord began. Most of the parkland lies along "Battle Road," the route of the British army's difficult and deadly retreat.

More than a million people come to the park each year. The visitors' center holds objects that reveal what life and war were like in the 1770s. Visitors can take a nearly six-mile trail that follows part of Battle Road. They can stop at places like Merriam's Corner or the Bloody Angle and see how the shape of the land affected the battles. At historic buildings in and near the park, park rangers and volunteers wearing clothes from the period tell the stories of the battles. They talk not only about the leaders but also of the ordinary people who were part of that historic day.

Americans have celebrated Paul Revere and other Patriots in artwork, poetry, and song. This sculpture of Paul Revere stands in Boston.

RELATED SITES

Visitors can see additional historic sites related to Lexington and Concord along the Freedom Trail in Boston. These sites include Paul Revere's home, which has been restored and turned into a museum. Near it stands the Old North Church, where the lantern signals were shown. The Old Granary Burial Ground includes the graves of Samuel Adams, John Hancock, and Paul Revere. The nearby cemetery of King's Chapel holds the grave of William Dawes.

Today, Massachusetts no longer celebrates Patriot's Day on April 19. Instead, the holiday falls on the third Monday in April. Still, Boston and nearby towns hold many events to remember the battles at Lexington and Concord. Reenactors dress in clothes and uniforms like those worn in 1775. Some reenact Paul Revere's ride and capture. Others act out the battles. Thousands of people come to the area each year to watch.

> *By the rude bridge that arched the flood, Their flag to April's breeze unfurled, Here once the embattled farmers stood And fired the shot heard round the world.*[15]
> —"Concord Hymn," Ralph Waldo Emerson, 1837

Modern-day reenactors, dressed as Redcoats, march toward the North Bridge in Concord.

TIMELINE

1763:   The French and Indian War ends with Britain defeating France.

1765:   The Sons of Liberty form in Boston to protest British taxes.

1770:   British troops kill five civilians in the Boston Massacre.

1773:   The Sons of Liberty destroy tea at the Boston Tea Party.

1774:   *March 30:* Parliament passes a law closing the port of Boston, the first of four Coercive Acts.

   May 17: General Thomas Gage arrives in Boston.

   September 5–October 26: The First Continental Congress meets in Philadelphia.

1775:   *April 18:* British troops leave Boston for Concord; Paul Revere and William Dawes begin their rides.

   April 19: British and colonial forces clash at Lexington and Concord.

   May 10: The Second Continental Congress begins meeting.

   June 17: The British drive the colonial forces from Breed's Hill in the Battle of Bunker Hill, the first major battle of the war.

1776:   The Second Continental Congress declares independence for the colonies.

1781:   The British army surrenders in Yorktown, Virginia, ending the last major battle of the American Revolution.

1783:   Britain recognizes American independence.

GLOSSARY

civilians—people who are not members of an organized military force

colony—an area controlled by another country, usually with settlers from the home country living and working in the colonized area for the benefit of the parent country

guerrilla warfare—irregular military tactics used by small bands of fighters

militia—a group of citizens organized for military service

minutemen—American colonists who promised to take up arms within a minute's notice

musket—a heavy, muzzle-loaded firearm, commonly used during the American Revolution

Parliament—the chief legislative body in Great Britain. Other nations also have parliamentary governments

reenactors—people who re-create historical events, often using authentic costumes and equipment

regular—a soldier in an official army, such as the British army in North America

reinforcements—fresh units sent in to strengthen troops in battle

FURTHER INFORMATION

BOOKS TO READ

Burgan, Michael. *Colonial and Revolutionary Times: A Watts Guide*. New York: Franklin Watts, 2003.

Fradin, Dennis Brindell. *Samuel Adams: The Father of American Independence*. New York: Clarion Books, 1998.

Hakim, Joy. *A History of Us: From Colonies to Country*. New York: Oxford University Press, 2002.

Nardo, Don. *The American Revolution*. San Diego: Lucent Books, 2003.

PLACES TO VISIT

Minute Man National Historical Park, Concord, Lincoln, and Lexington, Massachusetts
www.nps.gov/mima

Paul Revere House, Boston, Massachusetts
www.paulreverehouse.org

WEBSITES

Library of Congress Lexington and Concord Website
http://memory.loc.gov/ammem/today/apr19.html

The Declaration of Independence
http://www.ushistory.org/declaration/index.htm

NOTES

1. Edmund S. Morgan, *Benjamin Franklin* (New Haven: Yale University Press, 2002), p. 163.
2. Christopher Hibbert, *Redcoats and Rebels: The American Revolution through British Eyes* (New York: Avon Books, 1990), p. 25.
3. Bernard Bailyn, *The Ideological Origins of the American Revolution* (Cambridge, MA: The Belknap Press of the Harvard University Press, 1967), p. 126.
4. Robert Middlekauff, *The Glorious Cause: The American Revolution, 1763–1789* (New York: Oxford University Press, 1982), p. 266.
5. David Hackett Fischer, *Paul Revere's Ride* (New York: Oxford University Press, 1994), p. 99.
6. Ibid, p. 109.
7. Ibid, p. 164.
8. William M. Hallahan, *The Day the American Revolution Began: 19 April 1775* (New York: Perennial, 2000), p. 30
9. Ibid., p. 32.
10. Hackett Fischer, *Paul Revere's Ride*, p. 204.
11. Ibid., p. 213.
12. Hallahan, *The Day the American Revolution Began*, p. 47.
13. Page Smith, *A New Age Now Begins*, vol. 1 (New York: McGraw-Hill, 1976), p. 489.
14. Hackett Fischer, *Paul Revere's Ride*, p. 233.
15. Sculley Bradley et al., eds., *The American Tradition in Literature*, 3rd ed. (New York: Norton, 1967), p. 1211.

INDEX